T0063924

DANGERS *of* FAMILIARITY

Mercy Ayorinde

authorHOUSE®

AuthorHouse™ UK
1663 Liberty Drive
Bloomington, IN 47403 USA
www.authorhouse.co.uk
Phone: 0800.197.4150

Published by AuthorHouse   10/23/2014

ISBN: 978-1-4969-8992-5 (sc)
ISBN: 978-1-4969-8993-2 (e)

Scripture quotations marked KJV are from the Holy Bible,
King James Version (Authorized Version). First published
in 1611. Quoted from the KJV Classic Reference Bible,
Copyright © 1983 by The Zondervan Corporation.

TABLE OF CONTENTS

INTRODUCTION

Several times before I gave my life to Christ I have been hearing people using the common idiom to correct someone especially when they behaved rudely or insult an elderly person. It says *"Equality is not the same as equity."* It simply means, if a child does have many new clothes like an elderly person, he cannot have enough old clothe like an elder.

When we are to interpret this in reference to relational behaviour between leaders and followers, Pastors and members, then one will see that it is a common problem that has put a lot of people under total blindness through the deceptive influence of the spirit of familiarity. Most times, people who ended up as rebel may not intends it at first, but as a result of familiarities, they turn out to start fighting and scattering what they had joined

In this book, I have tried as much as possible to simplify the meaning, and the danger of familiarity.

ACKNOWLEDGEMENT

Thanks are unto the Almighty God for the inspiration for this book. And I heartily express my gratitude to those whom God has assigned to work towards the printing of this book.

I say to my son in the Lord, Rev. Kunle Adeoye thank you for given this work attention at the early stage and to Rev. Falaki Ola-Olu Sam, than you for making this vision a reality.

My special thanks go to my dear husband, Prophet (Dr.) Samson Ayorinde for his understanding, love and care. Dare, thank you sir, for every push and encouragement. You are truly a darling and a mentor.

I also appreciates all my Jewels, may the good Lord bless you all Amen.

DEDICATION

This book is dedicated to the true disciples of our Lord Jesus all over the world. Please be encouraged and remain steadfast to the end.

INTRODUCTION

I was on my face before the Lord one faithful day when He spoke into my heart some key words which I quickly got up to write down. I was in kind of dialogue in my spirit with the Lord during which my heart bled as the clarity of the message dawn on me. I found many young and upcoming ministers had actually laboured in the work of the kingdom of God and when they are so close to having good result, they become impatient and before you know it, they have entered into error. *I pray that you will never be a victim of the spirit of error*

Instead of harvest, many had ended up living under curses and spell. Then everything become hard and it appear they do not know how to do anything right again. It was while meditating on this that the Lord spoke into my heart, *"Daughter, a lot of children put too much attention trying to avoid attack from the spirit of fornication, adultery, anger etc. Yet many of them forget that there are other deadly strategies of the devil against the saints in the end time. Such deceptive innovations includes; Familiarity, Hypocrisy, Ego, Un-forgiveness and careless Living. Therefore, intercede and counter these subtle devices of the devil"*

The Lord said to me that the Saints of God are afflicted with 5 spiritual ailments:

(1) Spirit of Familiarity
(2) Spirit of Hypocrisy
(3) Spirit of Pride
(4) Spirit of Un-forgiveness
(5) Gossip – which is cause by I–too-know (Over Confidence)

That was what brought about the burden to put down this book. I therefore advice that you read this book carefully for it will open your eyes to certain basic truth. It is the truth that you know that can set you free. When you know how to halt demonic strategies around you, then you will be able to fulfill you God given destiny.

Do not allow the spirit familiarity to start telling you at this point that you do not need to read this book if you have read it to this line then strive to finish it through.

Shalom

WHAT IS FAMILIARITY?

The Longman Activist Study Dictionary defines familiarity as: a good knowledge of something, a relaxed feeling or way behaving because you know a person or place (too) well. In this context the 'second' definition serves our purpose.

Familiarity then is to have personal knowledge or information of or on or about a thing, environment, or a person. For example, you can be used to a tool that you can maneuver it as you desire. You can get so familiar with your environment that you can walk around in darkness. With people, the level of your acquaintance can be such that your respect and admiration for them diminishes. This does not necessary imply verbal abuse of the person(s). It rather suggested that you have become so accustomed to them that you no longer hold them in high regard or esteem.

Familiarity is the greatest blockage to tapping into or benefiting from the anointing of a vessel of God. It blocks the result of prayer and fasting.

Familiarity is an enemy of the believer just as procrastination is the coffin of success. Many children of God suffer from the demon or spirit of familiarity. They tend to take it for granted that they know the vessel or leader only too well which may lead to contempt. If the spirit of familiarity is afflicting your life; you should work on getting delivered and then free from it. It is just working on yourself and be determined be disciplined.

This is the reason the Bible says that: first shall be the last and the last shall be the first. Why should it be so?

The first become the last because the first is already accustomed to the way and manner things are done spiritually hence is relaxed. The last, having thirst for improvement eventually overtakes and become the first. This is because overtaking is allowed in the kingdom work

The spirit of familiarity robs us of power of God and the move of the anointing. It causes spiritual leakage in the life of saints leading to attack upon their souls by demons and eventually spiritual death. *Matthew 25, this is a story Jesus the Master told us Himself about the spirit of familiarity in action. The persons in this story are the 10 virgins – meaning the 10 were saints, they were saved and probably speaking in tongues. The 10 virgins are all the brides of Jesus and Jesus is their groom. It is expected that a bride should know key things her groom. Things like, when he goes out and when he will likely be back. In this story, these 10 virgins were probably used to the bride-groom movements, his intimacy, and just needed to wait for some few hours more for the groom to arrive. Ordinarily, a groom should not get distracted by anything when going to a date with his bride. So, the 5 virgins could not see any reason why the groom should not come to time. They were too familiar with the groom. They know that the groom love and care so much about them that he will not just keep them waiting. But the other 5 virgins though were sure of the love and care of the groom, refused to take anything for granted. Though they also known their groom too well still took extra oil, in case some issues come up and the groom has to extend his time of arrival. So, they took extra oil with them that they will have enough to keep waiting for the groom anytime he choose to arrive. Those other 5 virgins who do not have provision for extension of time ran short of oil. It was when they felt they should go look for extra oil, assuming that the groom will not mind waiting for them to return from their purchase. They thought he will certainly wait for us. After all we have been waiting for him too. Familiarity made them to neglect simple protocol. They became un-official in their dealings with the groom. When the spirit of familiarity is operating, protocols are not followed, we are not official and in this we cannot get things officially through.*

THINGS THAT PEOPLE
GET FAMILIAR WITH

he Word of God

Saints sometimes get so acquainted with the word of God that it loses its meaning to them and makes no difference in their lives. The WORD of God should bring life and healing to the hearer. The Word of God is His promise and counsel for us but whenever we got too familiar with the word, it remains a logo. Familiarity will not make the Word Rhema, and until it becomes a Rhema, it cannot be digested by the spirit. The Rhema make you to have an encounter, a personal experience that changes your life for good.

Some demons get so familiar with the atmosphere of the Word that they refuse to leave their victim. Act 16:16 says *"And it come to pass, as we went to prayer, a certain damsel possessed with a spirit of divination met us, which brought her master much gain by soothsaying"*. The lady was with Paul, so she heard the word and she was familiar with it and also with the people of God. However, on this occasion the Holy Spirit deliberately pointed her to Paul.

Beloved of God, have you become so conversant with the Word of God that it no longer moves you? The Word of God is so powerful for healing, for deliverance from sin, but despite God's obvious warnings, many still play with many of the vices recoded in the Bible. Why is it so? It is familiarity with the Word of God

The spirit of familiarity dries up the spirit of the fear of God in our heart. You can be a church leader who is so familiar with the word of God; God had become your usual style that you do not care to stay closer to God or His Word any longer. You have forgotten that the word of God is new every morning. No matter the extra time you spent in meditation, the Word of God comes new and fresh every time you read it. Creative and constructive inspirations and illumination come in deeper and fresher every day.

The Word of God is not what you can get too familiar with; you will need it in all your ways to lighten your path. *"Thy word is a lamp unto my feet, and alights unto my path" Ps119:105*. There is nothing you desire that is not in the Word of God. The Word gives you a voice; it is a sure foundation that you can build your trust on. Nothing can stop the Word from achieving its target either physical or spiritual. It gets through any obstacle on its path.

The Word of God is unique and knows no boundary. It cut across all over the world. It cannot be resisted to a nation, tribe or race. There is nothing you can do to stop the power of the Word of God. All a man need to get to a place of fulfillment in life is the Word. So, if you take the Word of God for granted, you will be grounded.

No matter how familiar you are with the Word, there is always freshness you can get out of it for your daily nourishment. You need the Word to survive just as a little baby needs the breast milk of the mother. Has it ever cross your mind that God is called the 'Breasted One', or ELSHADAL. EL, Meaning the Strong one and Shadai, meaning the Breasted One.

These compound name then place God as the 'Loving Mother', who has enough breast milk that everyone will suck to get nourished, fed satisfied, and fulfilled. You cannot afford to play with Word of God through familiar spirit. There is always freshness wisdom for living, and new inspiration. If you actually wants to success in life and have good success, the known key to it in the Bible is to meditate in the Word of God daily. The word you know create the world around you

Jos: 1:8 This book of law shall not depart out of thy mouth; but thou shalt meditate therein day and night, that thou mayest observe to do according to all that is written therein: for then thou shalt have good success.

God gave this secret to Joshua and repeated the same for emphasis sake. This is because the Word has an inner or hidden power in it that has the ability to bring about the success you so desire. Your ability to meditate in the Word is the determining factor of your level of success. So, do not get familiar with the Word to a point where you develop a thick skin for it.

There may also be someone in your church that is a great vessel in the hand of the Lord in the ministration of the Word, but he is criticized instead of being encouraged. Why? It is all a function of the demon of familiarity. This is what has made many of us no to appreciate the vessels of God around us.

The spirit of familiarity causes a person to utter derogatory word and statement about his leader thus underrating the grace of God upon his life. Unfortunately for such people, God will always fight on behalf of his servant and as such leader begins to rise, the slanderers will be going down. This is a spiritual principle.

As we will read further in the Bok of Numbers 12, although Moses did a wrong thing, Miriam had no right to accuse him hence she was punished for doing so because the judgment or the discipline of a leader is in the hand of God. However, most saints take over from God because of familiarity. Familiarity causes a person to cross his/her boundaries. It convinces you that you are doing the right thing after all you know the all the scripture and you are anointed too. Avoiding this spirit is a serious task for any Christian that wants to go far in life and ministry.

Remember Mariam was the same bold and intelligent young girl that stood by the basket that carried Moses along the shore of river Nile. Even when their mother had let go and returned home, Miriam kept watching until destiny brought the princess. So she was too familiar with Moses as his "little" brother. She allow familiarity into her relationship with Moses. This action made her the only lady in the Bible recorded to experience leprosy, and also caused serious retrogression or delay during the exodus for a whole NATION. When you are over familiar with a servant of God you are playing with leprosy and the spirit of retrogression or stagnancy. It is this generation that you will see people (believers and unbelievers alike) talking evil of the servants of God. This is a total indiscipline. In those days you see our aged parents who were as old as 60, 70, or even 80 years caring and honouring their pastor or any servant of God.

I have some brother–in–laws who are also men of God but never allow the office of the wife that I occupy in the family to tamper with the office I occupy as the wife of the General Overseer or a spiritual mother. They refuse to allow this kind of spirit to hinder them in our day to day relationship. You can also escape the subtlety of this demon whose aim is to gradually lead people to damnation. What exactly do you gain from running down your leaders or pastor?

The man you called a father a moment ago because you saw him as a mentor and a counselor, only for you to now crucify him the next moment. Why would you say '**Hosanna**' now and latter begin to shout crucify him? The only thing that can cause you to do that is familiarity, because you have known much enough about him that can be used to crucify him just like Judas Iscariot.

Dangers of Familiarity

Judas knew Jesus so closely enough to know precisely the place he will be at a particular time, and how to find him at Gethsemane thus he could betrayed him with a kiss. Unless you are very purposeful, it is very easy for this spirit to get into even the sincere ones unaware. So, be warned.

This demon is actually one of the causes of spiritual barrenness. The moment a follower begin to say negative thing about his leader or pastor, he will begin to experience dryness. This is just because in the spirit he has rebelled against a constituted authority for the scripture says that 'the rebellious dwells in the desert'. In the desert fruitfulness is rare.

Everything will now stand still in his spiritual life simply because when a man looses the blessing of the father, things will start to work against him. Things become very tight, your anointing start to leak and favour takes an immediate flight out of your life. Most spiritual benefit you used to enjoy now seems unreachable and you start to experience barrenness.

I suppose when spirit like failure, disappointment, delay, fornication, adultery, lying etc. come knocking on your door, you will definitely not welcome them talk less of entertaining them because you know as a child of God to have such things in you is sinful . So, what the devil does is to repackage these in more subtle forms. As familiarity or pride or unforgiveness or hypocrisy and lack of self-control. Now that you are getting aware of this demon spirit of familiarity you will do well to stay clear of it before it lure you into self-destruction.

God can overlook the weakness of a person he calls and uses, yet you, being one with faults too should not on to the fault of your leaders to crucify him for it. Remember that *Galatians 6-7 says* **"do not be deceived, god cannot be mocked. A man reaps what he sows."** That's why I respect the Joshua so much despite all he knew about Moses he never allow himself to be a victim of familiarity no wonder God noised him. Joshua 6:27. This is a spiritual law. Be careful, so that when you attain a position of leadership, your followers too will not behave in the manner you have behaved to your own leadership in the past.

The point is that; it is easy to fall prey into the deceptive claw of this demon. There was a time we went for a crusade in a town where my husband Prophet Ayorinde was raised up, and a man shouted from the crowd, 'Samson, Samson! You mean you are now a man of God. Wonderful!

This old colleague obviously must have remember when my husband used to go around the place without shoes and sent out of school for not paying tuition fees etc. it would be impossible for such a person to receive any blessing through my Husband except Gods intervention. This is because all he could still see was Samson Ayorinde of then, but the man ministering now is a great vessel in the hand of God.

When the familiar spirit take hold of your life, you will notice that you notice that you begin to gossip about your leader and assassinating his or her character. You no longer get blessed when they preach; you begin to mark his or her English whenever he opens his mouth to speak. You will even begin to finish off a statement for him before he says anything, and start rubbishing the testimonies that follow his ministrations.

When this demon takes possession, there is the tendency to start comparing your leader with others. You no longer bothered about sowing into your leader's life and ministry because you now see him or he as just like any other person in the church. Before now, you used to believe that there is a great reward in sowing into the life of your leader as the Bible says *'he who received a prophet in the name of a prophet get the prophet's reward'.* But is he stills your prophet?

Sometime you may feel like going to another church because you are no longer blessed by your leader's message and ministration. This is a sign that the demon has gotten hold of you. It is time to fight back for your soul. Escape from this demon before it destroys you if you do not act fast and stop its influence on you then it will invariably stop you. So, act now!!

It is also interesting to note that some people had all the opportunity to disrespect their leaders but they still did not. These are people who have seen their leaders moment of weakness, strength, triumphs and trials etc. yet they refused to give in to the demon of familiarity. If many of us Christian today were to be in the shoes of David in those days, the opportunity that came up in the cave of Adullam would have been the time we have been waiting for to end it all with our enemy – Saul the king.

Instead David still honour and defended the territory of Soul. You are steadfastly defended, respect and admire your leader. Look up to him or her as a role model and mentor. You should always see your leaders as a rare gem. Satan known that you are free from the obvious spirit such as idolatry, adultery, fornication etc. and so will certainly look for another way to get to you. Be on guard. Do not allow him to contaminate you with the same weakness that got him into his original mess. He got so familiar with God's glory that he thought it was something he could usurp. Beloved, as you work on this area, I pray that the hand of God Almighty will help you to remain steadfast in Christ, in Jesus name.

Thy word have I kept in my heart that I may not sin against you. You need to keep the word of God continually in your heart is the only way that keeps you away from sin and sin away from you.

In Acts. 5:1-5, Ananias died of shock when he knew that what he had done secretly was known and bare to peter. He was not particularly acquainted with the gift of the Word of knowledge hence his surprise at Peter disclosing hi secret deed. What happened in the days of the apostles in terms of the demonstration of the gift of the Spirit is still happening today even on a greater dimension yet people and churches are not benefiting from it as a result of familiarity.

People are becoming extremely used to these gifts such that it has become like soldiers sees wearing bullet proof as part of the uniform for war front. The proof is to wade off any direct effects from bullets. It is like manner that some saint are adorned with sermon proof garment which do not let the word of God have impact on them. Do not ever get to a state in your Christian life when the word of God will be like just any book to you. Always give the word its right place because in it is divine health, protection, prosperity, breakthrough etc. for you.

The Name of Jesus

Jesus and the People

Familiarity also occurs with the way we use the name of Jesus. Sometimes you call the name and it seems like it has lost its potency. The reason it appear so is because people call the name of Jesus but are guilty of lying, slandering, gossiping, backbiting, stealing etc.

Jesus on the Cross

We call the name of Jesus with our mouth and still destroy one another, especially those that are our leader with the same mouth and we are expecting God to honour what we ask for. No. we are the ones that gone astray and left the covenant name of Jesus. Today if you call the name of Jesus in righteousness, there is in it power to save and to deliver.

We get all our victory from the name of Christ when we are His own and keep to His terms. Do not be like the seven sons of Sceva who were not part of the family but got to using the name of Jesus only to attract harms to themselves. *The name of Jesus is so powerful that at the mention of the name alone every kneel must bow and all tongue must confess the Lordship of this mighty name of Jesus. This same name is powerful as a strong tower that whosoever runs into this name is SAVED.*

Familiarity In Prayer

Some men praying with Mummy G,O
on the Mountain Top

Imagine someone whose phone started ringing while praying, and then stop praying to give attention to pick up only to come back later to continue prayer.

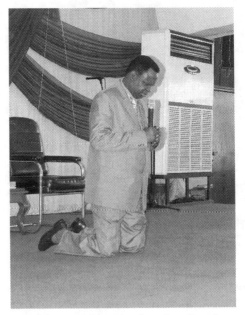

Daddy Kneeling on the altar Praying

Would any citizen in a conversation with a governor or better still a president stop to pick up his or her phone when it rings? People will readily obey orders to swift to switch off their phones before having audience with the president or governor but we take the time spent in prayer before God the president of presidents for granted. People do all sorts of things when they are praying. Excising or ding other activities and speaking in tongues, chew gums, greet a passer – by and other chores while praying.

If you had an hour to spend, would it not be better to spend 30 minutes out of I hour with God and the rest 30minutes on other things you have to do instead of doing them at the same time together? Some will have a petition with God and will be chewing gum; can you dialogue with all seriousness as you chew? It is now a common sight that people come to the church, the place of worship and meeting with God very casual and indecently dressed. They forget that the way you are dressed is the way you will be addressed.

Watch out if you have found yourself doing things this way either knowingly or unknowingly. You should have a consciousness of how to relate with God and your choice of words when you are speaking to Him. Even though God is love, we should not take Him for granted because He is sovereign and His sovereignty must be upheld and respected. Remember, if you take God for granted, you will be grounded. May the Lord help us.

Crowd praying

The Blood of Jesus

Ezekiel 36:25 "I will sprinkle clean water on you and you will be clean, I will cleanse you from all your impurities and from all your idols"

Revelation 12: 11 "they overcome him by the blood of the lamb and by the word of their testimony; they did not love their lives so much as to shrink from death"

The blood of Jesus is another powerful weapon provided for our victory over the power of darkness. As a continuous witness to the power of the blood, Christ commanded us to keep a steady remembrance of His sacrifice. Luke 22:17 – 19 Says:

Luk 22:17 and he took the cup, and gave thanks, and said, take this, and divide it among yourselves:

Luk 22:18 For I say unto you, I will not drink of the fruit of the vine until kingdom of God shall come.

Luk 22:19 And HE took Bread, and gave thanks, and brake it and gave unto them, saying, This is my body which is given for you; this do in remembrance of me.

Through the blood of Jesus our salvation is complete. Ask Him to cleanse you with His blood. Surrender to Jesus and believe in the blood shed for you.

The blood of Jesus is so powerful that it cannot be comprehended by the power of darkness when they encounter it. It never loses its power. It never clots and it is eve fresh every day. It is to give you victor in your battles. Nevertheless, familiarity with communion service can make a man to lose the benefit of the effectiveness of the blood working for us. Through our ministry, I have come in contact with people who view the communion as refreshment; needless to say, they receive it and do not see or get desired result. Please do not become familiar with the blood of Jesus and the sacrifice He made on the cross of Calvary for you and me. Remember it cost Him his dear life. What a great sacrifice He made for us.

I remember a sister in our ministry who refused the communion, I asked her why, 'oh you should have taken it for your deliverance', I said, and she replied me with sarcastic laughter and said 'you sound so serious, is it not just ordinary wine?' That is exactly what I'm saying! To some the blood of Jesus is an ordinary wine, while some others see it as a contact point to get healing and deliverance.

For those who sees it as a wine, oh! What a wonderful style of entertainment; very refreshing. But for those who take it in faith as the BLOOD of Jesus Christ, it does wonderful works of healing, deliverance, favour, and it is a cup of blessing. To the regenerated ones, we thank God for the efficacy of Blood of Jesus.

There was this incredible experience in one of our communion service, when a woman suddenly screamed of stomach pain after receiving the Communion. Immediately, she saw blood stain on her cloth, and she rushed to the hospital. Later on that same day, without her going through any surgical operation, a sizeable fibroid came out of her by the power in the blood of Jesus.

In the life of so many children of God, this precious blood has been wonderful in its manifestations. The blood of Jesus when implored upon a place brings sanity and liberty. The mark of the blood on the lintel of the Hebrew in the land of Goshen was what separated them from death and calamities. The angel of death could not come into their house. They had a wonderful time of peace and protection while their counterpart in Egypt could not escape that night from the agony of death. That is what the Blood of Christ stand for. You too can get connected into this same power in the blood even now. It's so powerful.

The Anointing Oil

Every oil remains an ordinary oil until it has been prayed upon then it becomes anointing oil. To understand the mystery of the anointing oil, we should be aware that God gave us dominion in the beginning. Genesis 1:28 declares;

And God blessed them, and God said unto them, be fruitful, and multiply, and replenish the earth, and subdue it: and have dominion over the fish of the sea, and over the fowl of the air, over every living thing that moveth upon earth. Saul was an ordinary man until the anointing oil separates him to be a champion over God's inheritance. In 1st Samuel 10 he was anointed with oil and in 1st Samuel 11 the special oil brought anger that made him to do exploit against king Nahash and his cabinet. King David was anointed with oil 3 different times, for 3 levels of operation in a divine way. Many times people bring oil to be prayed upon, and some even sent it overseas and miracles of healing, deliverance and gift of babies are recorded.

This dominion was lost when Adam fell. Genesis 3:17 – 19 says

Gen 3:17 And unto Adam he said Because thou hast hearkened unto the voice of thy wife, and hast eaten of the tree, of which I commanded thee saying, Thou shalt not eat of it : cursed is the ground for thy sake; in sorrow shall thou eat of it all the days of thy life;

Gen 3:19 Thorns also and thistles shall it bring forth to thee; and thou shalt eat the herb of the field;

Gen 3:19 In the sweat of thy face shalt thou eat bread, till thou return unto the ground; for out of it wast thou taken: for dust thou art, and unto dust shall thou return.

This lost dominion was restored back to us by Jesus Christ on the cross of Calvary. So we now have dominion if we are in Christ. The Bible also declares in Mattew16:18 that *"and I say also unto thee, that thou art peter and upon this rock I will build my church; and the gates of hell shall not prevail against it."*

This is the assurance that we have as believer that if the saint join their faith together and pray on oil and send it to the sick or the oppressed through a representative of the church, the Bible assures us that they shall be healed and even if they had sinned they shall be made whole James5:14. We ought to respect this Word of God as regard the use of anointing oil.

Psalm 92:10 talks about how you have the emblem of excessive strength and favour of God you have been anointed with oil.

In 2nd King 4: 1 – 5, we read the story of a man of God who was greatly indebted when he died. If the man of God had not been using oil there would have been no oil in their house. And without it, his family would have remained in debt and his children would have been taken away into slavery by creditors. Anointing oil is to be used positively but some people have gone under certain teachings which had resulted into its misuse.

Some people now applied anointing oil to kill cockroaches that disturbs them in their house even after killing them. Some will even robbed it all over their body because they feel guilty after committing fornication or adultery. This is an abuse of the power deposited in that oil. The sacredness placed on the use of the anointing oil will loose the power when the spirit of familiarity is at work through sin. The anointing oil separate you for greatness, desire the anointing of oil.

Anointing oil bottles

Daddy Praying on Anointing oil

Samuel Anointing Saul

The same thing applies to blessed water. The fact is that the moment you abuse the access you have to sacred material and people of God who are bestowed with such power, familiarity set in. it removes the fear and respect of God along with the anointing in that material that make work wonders in the first place. It ceases to work because that which makes it to work has been abused. Such abuse comes as a result of familiarity. There is every tendency to abuse what you are used to or familiar with.

The Servant of God

The man of God you become familiar with cannot discipline you when you offend in the church. Children of God our days can never allow discipline especially when they fall into sin of fornication, adultery, steeling etc. why? (a) Self Ego (b) What people will say about them, people gossip about them (c) people will no longer trusts me that I will not do such again (d) Everybody hate me! (e) Where will I start again?

Every of this point is true but it depends on your focus on the eternal. To make heaven it costly you know? It will surely cost you self-denial, self-sacrifices, boldness, and great determination, if not you will keep looking at what people will say or feel etc. You will stop looking to the way of the cross and look down to self which can make you to loose out. Remember that is the main purpose of the devil. He lost out with God, lost his position and so his aim is that every other person should miss it too.

When you offend and church disciplines you, the best is to serve your discipline, and then remain. So that in the same place where you receive humiliation is where you will be honoured. Whatever is up will soon come down, and whatever is hot will soon become cold. So have courage and serve your punishment so that it can be well with you.

It is not good to offend the church of God. When you walk out of the church of God, it is disrespecting to the people of God and anything you do against the church of God, God does not take it likely. It makes you to become unsettled spiritually. It makes you to be a vagabond Christian. Stay focus it makes you to have a better testimony. The rebellious stay in the desert - desert is a day place of no life. When you walk away from the church, it makes you dry, you are spiritually unhealthy.

Picture of a Desert

The man of God you become too familiar with may not be a source of inspiration to you. Try as much as possible to ensure that your closeness to a man of God does not in any way diminish your respect or admiration for him. Be careful. The moment the spirit of familiarity sets in between you and a servant of God, you begin to dry up slowly and then spiritual death will follow sooner or later. When you get close to a man or woman of God, you can love them, pray for them, listen to them, encourage them, and then get blessed by them, yet you must not disrespect them else you will loose out of the grace of God upon their live.

Apostle Paul & Timothy

Elijah and Elisha

WEBIC MINISTERS

This is a direct warning to all young servants of God; do not allow the subtle demon of familiarity to block the flowing of grace and anointing into your live from your leaders. Do not be the one that will point to the people the weakness of your leader. There is no man that is perfect, and if you have one that says he is, then he is above the usage of God. God does not look for the perfect man to use but He is a specialist in getting the imperfect man to be a great vessel in His hands.

Moses & Joshua

12 spies

When you notice that you are beginning to point at the weakness of your leader it is a sure sign of familiarity. You ask yourself; why didn't talk about his or her weakness before? It was because the demon of familiarity was far from you, but now that it has entered you, it will facilitate your criticism and confrontation and my candid advise is that you flee from familiarity and refuse to give it an abode in your heart because the moment you allow it to get you focus on fault finding, then your source of inspiration and strength is closed. And just like a closed tap, very soon the water will definitely stop flowing to you no matter how many day of prayer and fasting you do to get it. The anointing you do not celebrated will not flow to or work for you.

There is no gainsaying that before the spirit of familiarity set in, you must have first loved your leaders in spite of their faults. Do not allow yourself to become possessed by this spirit of self-destruction, instead use whatever fault s you think you have discovered to get to a higher level than they have. The weakness that you see in them should be a guide to you, use it to learn and come out more refined.

As an intimate follower of a leader, there is no how you will not see his weakness but you are to allow love to cover his multitude of "sin" (weaknesses). If you do this, you will see yourself loving him with his fault. Remember you have some faults too and one day you will be greatly anointed 1st Cor 13:6 – 8

"Love does not delight in evil but rejoices with the truth. It always protects, always trusts, always hopes,

and always perseveres. Love never fails. But where there are prophecy's, they seas; where there are tongues, they will be stilled; where there is knowledge, it will pass away".

Love never fades; it makes you to accept the weakness of your Leader.

Again be careful not to abuse spiritual authority. See Number 12:2-16. God was not taking side with Moses, though what Moses did was considered wrong going by the same law that he brought to the people from God, yet God will never put the rod of discipline of His servant (Generals) into the hand of the sheep.

This was the same thing that happened with Jesus, He was not respected in His own town. To some He was just the carpenter's son, but to me He is my Lord and Saviour of my soul. When He noticed the familiarity expressed by people around Him, He asked the disciples, 'who do men say that I am' and 'who do you say I am.' As for Judas Iscariot, Jesus' worth is equivalent to about thirty shekel. He sold Saviour of the World for a few coins. What about you? Who is Jesus to you?

Familiarity also breeds disloyalty. People become easily disloyal, disrespectful, and dishonest when they are possessed with the spirit of familiarity. Familiarity creates strife, jealously and carnality. It attract death warrant that makes you become rebel. When you wear the shoes of rebellion, you see yourself fighting against your leaders in your heart. It then progresses to thinking you can do thing better than him or her.

You can cover or defend the weakness in your leader. People do this easily in the corporate world of business, companies, industries and some organization. It can be done in mission/church too.

The next thing is that you start to say negative and derogative things about him and your following action will be nothing less than exposing him or her to the whole world if you happen to know of any weaknesses about him. When you do this it results into death. A lot of people (ministers) who are walking on the street today are actually dead spiritually because they are rebels. This is another reason why the power of God is not in great manifestation in this generation as expected.

Rebels dry up gradually, their joy can never be full, and they lived under fear and torment before they will eventually die even physically. The spirit of rebellion enters easily through the spirit of familiarity. This is the reason why I kept on repeating it that you need to be on guard. Do not be deceived.

Absalom running away from David

The fact that a man does not impress you does not mean he does not impress God. God in His infinite mercies will continue to use a man even when men had concluded that he is not fit for God's great work. Your incessant complaints cannot stop God move of Grace upon a man. Who will ever give Moses, an ex-convict and a murderer, a chance considering his level of anger and his marriage to an Ethiopian woman? Yet, God still called him and was with him all through his days with the children of Israel.

If you find yourself in a position where all of a sudden you become opposite to the style, vision and ministry of your leader, then you are in a great danger. Rebellion is already standing by your side and this is dangerous for you. Samuel 6:20. It is your responsibility to shield and protect your leader always. Believe in him, pray for him on his area of weakness, cover his nakedness, and love him. Never you conceive the idea that your leader cannot offend you? The truth is that, the closer you are to him, the more of him you will see.

No body just wakes up to become a traitor or a slanderer who one way or the other has not yielded first to the spirit of familiarity. Remember it takes a close person to become familiar with someone. Psalm 41:9.

Psa 41:9 *Yea, mine own familiar fried, in who I trusted, which did eat of my bread, hath lifted up his heel against me.*

Familiarity can rear its ugly head anytime but it takes spiritual discipline not to fall into its hands because people will always takes things for granted when given the opportunity.

There was a day I was traveling with one of the members of staff, I was trying to meditate on the message I was going to preach and she started to sing, even though they were Christian songs, I corrected her and told her that she becoming too familiar for that was out of protocol.

If you notice that you how are beginning to address your boss, pastor or leader as you wish and feel no remorse afterwards, then you should watch it,

Speaking in Tongues

Crowd praying in the church during
72 Hours Before the Lord

This gift and the evidence of the indwelling of the Holy Spirit is also one thing that people takes for granted especially when we are familiar with Holy Spirit. Some people, after their sinful act of fornication and adultery will state to speak in tongues to quickly check if the Holy Spirit is still there or not. Without any doubt, we have heard many of them who still flow very well after had done such evil deeds. This is because the bible say's 'for God gift and his call are irrevocable' Romans 11:29.

Rom 11:29 for the gifts and calling of God are without repentance.

Though one may be speaking in tongues but the power in the manifestation of the spirit gradually fades out.

This is why speaking in tongues these days is not the evident of a godly living. So always ask yourself this question, 'is there still power of the Holy Spirit behind the tongue that I speak?

Your Spouse

With couple in suit & gown

Couples in native

Daddy passing his Mantle (Agbada) to
Mummy for empowerment on some set of
new ministers

Though this point is coming last here yet it is a major problem among even the saint. You are the closest person to your spouse and so you know all his or her weaknesses. You can always guess what his or her next line of action or behaviour is, yet you must not get too familiar with him or her else this will breed disrespect and if he is a servant of God. You may even begin to find it difficult to recognize the grace of God upon his life. See your spouse as a rear gem, a great vessel in the hands of God every time. If you do this you will continuously get blessed around him

To all women out there who happen to be wives of General Overseer or pastors, be very careful I had an encounter sometimes ago when we were running four to five services on a Sunday before we now decentralized into branching. After attending two or three of the service I decided to get into the office attending to other ministerial issues.

This continued until one day I suddenly felt the presence of the Holy Spirit and He was telling me to be careful of familiarity. I quickly apologize and ran out of my office to join the service. In His sovereignty, he forgave me because I was greatly blessed that day. It is a privilege to be a man of God's wife. Let's honour the office.

General Overseers wives

Since that time, I attend all services and whoever wants to see me will have to wait or book an appointment for another day. I cannot take the Holy Spirit or His vessels for granted.

In the Bible, Michal, the wife of king David took him for granted when her husband was actually praising his God. She paid for it dearly as she remained barren all her life. 2nd Samuel 16:16-23

Her problem started not on that day. She was already too familiar with her husband, the king, that she does not recognize the anointing on him anymore. David was not just her husband; he was the king over the people and a prophet too. He must represent his people before God. David was a servant of God and so he must ministered unto the Lord. David was a worshipper of the Almighty God and so must express his faith continually before him. Michal was indeed blinded to all these because of the issue of pride and familiarity.

I remember some year ago when a woman said to me, 'you honour so much or (respect) your husband too much, 'and I simply responded that 'yes I learnt it from Sarah.'

1st Peter 3:6 "for after this manner in the old time the holy women also, who trusted in God, adorned themselves, being in subjection unto their own husband: Even as Sarah obeyed Abraham, calling him lord: whose daughter ye are, as long as ye do well,. And are not afraid with amazement."

The only occasion that Sarah even took her husband decision for granted brought about a serious trouble in the family the effect of which we are still facing up till today. Often times, wives of men of god become victims of the spirit of familiarity. They say things like, 'if no one will correct you, I will.' Or "if no one can say anything about you, I can' etc.

I want wives of men of God to realize the sensitivity of their position particular if your husband is a Prophet. *Do not throw caution* to the wind whenever you are speaking to your husband because the sword in his mouth is not a respecter of persons or status. Michal, David's wife was guilty of this even though she must have very intimacy with him yet she was not spared.

The more anointing your husband is, the more careful you have to be. You should not react any how towards a man of God because you are his wife or a relative lest you wear the same shoe that people like Miriam and Michal wore.

To avoid this I am cautions not to disrespect my husband or play with word from him. If anybody now think that, 'I fear him or respect him' too much it is their own problems not mine. In all I make sure that I do not offend the God of the Prophet.

Once again, be careful of familiarity; remember that extreme closeness to someone may easily lead to diminished admiration and respect for them. As a matter of fact, respecting and honouring any servant of God around you whether he is your husband or not is what you must strive to do. Watch out! The spirit of familiarity is a spiritual killer and destroyer of anointing. It leaks power away, and it quenches the flame until the fire in you is put off. It also destroys good relationship and breed hatred.

Familiarity as a spirit is a silent kill in the spirit realm or in spiritual matters just like hypertension or high blood pressure in a silent killer in the physical or health wise.

TRAITS OF FAMILIARITY

I t is easy to detect familiarity spirit when it starts to manifest in a person. Read through the point and do a self-check or self-appraisal to see if you are also getting ensured already. And if you are, it is time that you do quick turnaround from such style of spiritual living that leads to leakages and spiritual deterioration.

Carefree Attitude Towards Those We Should Hold In High Esteem

People who have been in the church for a very long time sometimes take the Lord and His servant for granted. This is one of the reason I love the military. I don't know if it is because of their training but they always give regards and respect to whom it is due and are always formal in addressing their formal in addressing their superior even when they are not on duty. If the physical soldiers do this, the spiritual ones should do no less.

Indifference And Withdrawal Of Service And Commitment

You begin to delay in going to church and sees worship time as secondary. You are no longer moved when worship team ministers. You withdraw from praises and worship. You see it as a period to pass tie or wait for late comer's and you begin to pass negative comment about the singer, their dressing and kind of music played, you no longer appreciated God in the service of other Christians around. Please understand that when you do not appreciated God you will definitely begin to depreciate.

Once you pastor messages no longer interest or excites you or the respect you used to have for his person is no longer there; at this point you will no longer crave to sit in the front row where you can offer your support to the fellowship, rather your withdrawal gets you to start feeling as if you are just been used. Beloved, you will need God's own mercy to break loose of the influence of the demon of familiarity. And my prayer is that the Lord in His mercy will not allow you to destroy by this evil spirit.

Lack of Excitement

Boredom sets in with the spirit of familiarity. You are used to every move of the spirit and so you then begin to come to the house of God reluctantly. Gradually, you begin to sleep during the service which is a direct indication of lack of excitement because you are just present bodily but was never part of the service. Sometimes you just walk into the church to mark your presence else people will begin to ask question which you are not ready to even answer. At this point only the Lord can help you.

Withdrawal of Gifts

The spirit of familiarity has obviously take deep root when people get to the point where they no longer see reason why they should bless or even sow into the congregation or the live of their leader. In event where they give, they do so without reverence and without the expectation of any reward. The Bible makes it clear that when you give a cup of water to the man of God you will receive the reward of a Prophet. Matthew 10:14.

The people who get so familiar with their pastors or leaders will not give to the man of God pasturing them but will gladly give to invited speakers. It is the same people that will also seek and call their pastor and leaders at odd hours for prayers. Please, do not get me wrong, it is not wrong to give to other ministers and ministries, neither is it wrong for you to call at odd time when the need arise but you should give to you home base ministers well enough too. It is said that charity begins at home.

When you notice that the only time you have the leading to sow is when another man of God preaches, then the spirit of familiarity is creeping in already on you. When you bless a man of God, he will appreciate it from the deepest part of his heart, and whenever he uses that thing or remembers your gift to him, it is also a reminder to God that your case or life needs to be visited. Note that it is not all gifted that the Lord accepts but I pray the Lord will accept your gift in Jesus name.

Never give a man of God gifts as precursor so as not to be admonished by him or to gain recognitions within the fold neither should it be to inspire him in praying for you. God is the searcher of all hearts and such gifts definitely have no reward with him

Loss of Interest In Reading Books And Literatures By Your Leaders

Pile of Books

Picture of CD's

Have you recently asked yourself why you hardly feel like reading your pastor's book or journals? It may well be that the spirit of familiarity has set in. think about it. Why is it that you no longer buy your pastor's books or tapes and CD's you buy those from other servants of God? You probably feel there is nothing more that your pastor has to add to you.

There was a day that one man of God was invited to our ministry to minister, and after his message I noticed that all the tapes and book he came with were rushed by the people to the extent that they had to struggled to keep one for his friend was not in the service, yet our own tape were on sales without anyone picking them.

As I ponder on this, the Holy Spirit whispered to me Daughter, what is your stress? That is the spirit of familiarity in action. They believe they will always hear their pastor but this visitor will be gone in a moment. When you go out to preach too, don't you see the way people are always craving to collect your books and asked for your phone number? The spirit of familiarity will make you to loose interest in your pastor books and tapes. It is the same everywhere that is why pastors have their material appreciated more by outsiders.

Adoption

When this spirit creeps in, the old members of the church start to act like they are members of your nuclear family. They act like adopted children, their language, actions and characters now show they are part of you. This should not be problem at all considering the fact that the blood that brought us together is ticker and more and more effective, truthful and reliable than any other source of relationship, but the people that find themselves in this category should not only be careful but be discipline. They are not allowed to step beyond their boundaries.

Before you know it, they may fall into the error of discussing personal life of their pastor or leader with other people who may have no genuine love for their leader. And when care is not taken they will talk out of order. It is easy for such people to release information about their leaders or pastor to critics who will use such information to run them down.

May who are closer to their leaders do this ignorantly. Initially they were only trying to show how close they were to the man of God but eventually betrayed them to the hand of critics. This will only make then to loose out at the end. Mark 6:3, 2nd Samuel 15, 16. Watch what you your mouth to say about your leader. All in the name that you have been adopted by the Pastor

Fault Finding

I am sure that you will agree with me that there are no perfect human beings on heart. Those of us that are saved by grace are only enjoying the benefits of salvation. We are justified by faith and not our good works. However, everybody expect pastors to be perfect. Those that should have understand along with some men of God and strengthen them in time of trials are the same people that are often used to find fault on them. When you begin to see the fault of a servant of God and use it against him, it is a sign that your lover for him has diminished. So cheek your love gauge. 1st Cor. 13:4-7.

For fault finders, it is like the initial love they had for their pastor had taken flight and flown away to unknown place. You should learn to know that your pastor is an ordinary man in the hands of a Great God who is using him to do great things. The truth is that by the time you get close to other men of God that you think are more nice that your own pastor out of familiarity, you will soon discovered that the relationship you had was a privilege and should not have been taken for granted.

So, what do you do when you are ensured by the spirit of fault finding? You start to intercede for your leaders. In the face of trials and tribulations. You have to accommodate their shortcomings. The more you do so, the more heavens will also be merciful upon you in the days of trials. Then you can call for twice the grace that God put upon him and God will definitely give it you.

Elisha commitment and dedication to Elijah in time of challenges kept him following even when other sons of prophets had backed out. No wonder he received the double portion of the anointing. David, despite the opportunities that he had to get rid of king Saul, did not make the mistake of attacking the Lords anointed. This was one of the many reasons God never allow the plots of other men prevail against him when he finally got to the throne. Joshua faithfully stood in for Moses despite the weakness of anger often demonstrated by Moses. This brought Joshua to the position of honour when he least expected

Nowadays, things are out rightly different. Followers who know their leaders weak point are often eager to push him off the peak. Those who could not even lay their hand on anything will not mind to fabricate one if that will clear the road for them. May the Lord of the church deliver this generation from the spirit of familiarity.

A man of God once shared his experience with me. One day, after he finished ministering to a stunted audience, a lady walked up to him and said; *"That was a very powerful ministration sir; but there were about 64 grammatical errors in your message."* This lady really would have been blessed if she had listened to the message and not to his grammar? She was only able to remember the error and not the blessing of her soul in the message. She forgot that God is not moved by our eloquent words but by the inspiration in the spoken word

Comparison

When familiarity has eaten a man up, he will begin to make comparism between leaders. That is when you will begin to notice how greedy, or inferior, or arrogant, or unfriendly your pastor or leader is. You immediately begin to see other people as been better than him. Before you know it you will start to make a round table talk with other immature mind around you. Immature because it takes a novice in spiritual thing to sit down around a table to discoursed his or her leaders and pastor. Any one already manifesting this kind of character is in great danger and needs immediate help.

You should always know that your leader is a man of like passion. Just a man like you. He has his own nature and temperament which may be as a result of upbringing or genetically make ups. Genetically he could either be a sanguine, choleric, phlegmatic, or melancholic. No matter how anointed a man is, these genetic make ups still play a major role in his life, *though anointed or not every one need to pray on their temperament because all temperament has both positive and negative effects.*

Nicknames

Have you ever heard some people calling their leaders or pastors by some funny nicknames? It is a mere disrespect which is developed overtime through familiarity. It makes follower to make mockery of their leaders. It makes members to negatively mimic their pastors. This is not proper, so desist from it if you already join team of mocker, mockers are just vision destroyers.

When you disrespect a servant of God while on duty, you may assume it is nothing but God is not taking it lightly at all. None of those children that mocked Elisha while returning from the mountain top did live again to tell the story thereafter. So be careful

Discussing Private And Family Life Of A Servant Of God

Whenever you do this, you automatically cut yourself from the source of power and presence of god. Sometimes ago, God gave me burden to pray for some leaders, pastors and ministers' wives. I have never been to the churches of some of them but I obeyed. I would mention their names and family members and uphold them in prayers. I discovered that when I finished this assignment I felt elated spiritually and it was like new oil flowing through my spiritual system. In essence, I believe that's the opposite will definitely happened if anyone makes negative pronouncement about a man of God. He get dried up and everything about him will start to nosedive.

1st Chronicles 16:19 – 22: When ye were but few, even a few and strangers in it.

1st Chronicle 16:20: And when they went from nation to nation, and from kigdom to another people;

1st Chronicles: 16:21 He suffered no man to do them wrong: yea, he reproved kings for their sake.

1st Chronicle: 16: 22. Saying, Touch not mine anointed and do my prophet no harm.

Therefore any gossip on a man of God causes spiritual leackages and eventual dryness, the more anointed the man of God is, the more dangerous and devastating the effect of the dryness

Disrespect

When the spirit of familiarity sets in, you no longer feel the need to heed to your leaders advice or take to your pastor's counsel. His words no longer appeal to you; he is now like every other person. The same people that will always want to hear his or her opinion before you accept his counsel if at all you will. And anytime you are asked to mention some respectable men of God, hardly will you remember to make mention of his name.

All you see about him are his weaknesses, corruption, disrespect and dishonor sets in. your focus is on the minor qualities of your leader. Read 1st Corinthians 15:42-43. Never take your pastor or leader for granted, rather embrace them even with their entire fault.

This is what the Lord did for His own pleasure and glory despite their weakness and fault. Romans 8:30, Revelation 4:11

Your pastor is also God sent so, honour your God's grace gift in him and this will naturally deal with the spirit of familiarity around you. When we read 1st Corinthians 12: 1-20, it is evident that Apostle Paul expects us to honour the grace of God upon each other for the purpose of expanding and strengthening the kingdom. All leaders cannot have the same gift and grace. The owner of the gift and grace distributes it as He pleases. Yours is to respect whosoever this grace is given to.

People are called to different offices, Ephesians 4:11. A person might be a prophet and a teacher while another will conveniently operates as a prophet and evangelist, each office comes with different levels of grace to enable individuals function and to perform. Matthew chapter 25 makes us to understand that God gave each of His children talents according to how He fined it fit. The man with one talent suffered as a result of familiarity.

Reading the scripture very well will help us to see that he already assumed that his master was nothing but a taskmaster. That made him to loose out. The same thing applied to the 10 virgins in the same book and chapter. The five wise ones, not being over confident of their master's schedule took extra oil with them. However, on the other hand, the foolish virgins assumed they knew the masters very well missed out. The Bible says that a kingdom that is divided against it-self will not stand, so stop saying derogative thing about your leaders.

Though there were a lot of men in the Bible who fell to the error of the spirit of familiarity. Lot, the nephew of Abraham is such men. The spirit of familiarity only bring demotion, barrenness, depression, frustration, suffering, distress and confusion while respect and hounor of your leaders will attract joy, promotion, happiness, fruitfulness and breakthrough. So make a choice today!

Discussing and Disrespecting

Discussing and disrespecting other Servant of God from other Churches and Ministry. God Almighty is not a respecter of person what I have found rampant in the body of Christ today is that some Christians believe that only their own pastor is anointed, good and must be honoured. Every other minister is not better than a swine to them. How? They gossip about other servants of God that is not their pastors and give evil report about such a pastor to their own pastor thereby staining their pastor relationship with the external pastor. They disrespect, dishonor and say evil things about the external pastor. Unfortunately, some pastors who are novice to the pranks of followers too believe them.

Jesus desire is that part of his palm and sacrifice on the cross is that we all should be one. The believers in the Book of Matthew, and those in the Act of the Apostles, even though they operated differently never run each down, neither did people around them run down their counterparts. I ask you as a believer why do you take the pleasure of running down other men of God to your own pastor, even if you feel that yours is the most anointed, he is the only good one, fine but you don't have to destroy or assassinate the character of others just because you want people to feel yours in the best.

In corporate companies, people don't do that, you can only advertise your product convincingly not that you will call a product and run it down or make a negative proclamation about such product. If you do, the other company will sue you to court. The same is also true in the spiritual business. The angels on assignment, who are commanded to be a support for that mandate, will "sue" you and even discipline you if need be. Unfortunately instead of you to think through on this, you will say it is an attack.

The Bible says **"touch not my anointed"**, he did not say touch not my anointed that is you pastor. God cannot have YOUR PASTOR ALONE to evangelize, deliver and pray for the whole world i.e why he has call others too and if you don't stop this your habit of running down other ministers to your pastor, God will discipline you Himself, because you are creating discord between his sons/daughters and He will not smile at that.

The record in the book of Genesis told us that Abraham and Lot had to separate and this ruined the destiny of Lot. Do you know that it was the people under Abraham and Lot that started the problem? Some people that work with servants of God has cause a great SEPARATION between their pastors and other pastors. In fact they choose who their pastor should relate with. Those that their pastors want and they don't want they run down to their pastor. God Almighty will not be pleased with such people. When you respect and honor 'collar' servants of God, heaven will reward you anywhere and any times, then heaven too will arrange your own honour divinely.

Do you know that what you use your mouth to say never leave the mind of the one you said it to? And he or she uses it against that man of God? I remember the 5 afflictions of saints as the Lord revealed to me sometimes ago. These are really affecting the ministerial unity and progress. They are: (I) Sprit of Familiarity (II) Spirit of Hypocrisy (III) Spirit of Pride (IV) Spirit of un-forgiveness (V) Spirit of Gossips.

Gossip is cause by I–too–know or over confidence which make you to run down other. The Egyptians midwives became landowners just because they FEAR GOD of the Hebrew Exo 1:20. God will build you houses, build your life and that of your children if you fear the God of Israel in the life of other men of God and believe that God of your own leader is also in their lives. Remember a kingdom should not be divided against itself. It is the same kingdom we belong, going to the same heaven, serving the same God. We have same savior, same Spirit, same faith! Why then do we ruin down each other's leader? Just because we have different name of churches/denomination – all these are man-made. Get to heaven, you will know.

Other religions don't run down their leaders. Even the evil people says "Awo lo n gbe awo ni gbowo" a spiritualist help each other even when they don't belong to the same leader.

CHRISTIAN THINK AND MEDITATE ON THIS. According to Gen 11, we can be more united and progressive if we love respect and honour each other more.

EXAMPLES

In Our ministry, I have been amazed by the character of some people I have come across. I will want to give three examples of such families who though were so close yet maintained a good and respectable rapport with the leadership.

Family A

This couple knew us when we had nothing. In fact, I was still a student in Ahmadu Bello University under his directorate. Eventually we became prayer partners and our ministry was later born. This man also became a full time minister in our ministry yet his regard and admiration for us never diminished.

Family B

A very elderly family in our church that has been very close in Television Ministry together, yet never disrespect us one day, always given us due honour and respect. With this, it is impossible for them to be victims of familiarity.

Family C

There is another family who has been our domestic staff for a very long time, meaning they had seen us when we were low and when we are high. They were with us when we were hungry and when we now have enough to eat. In spite of this, they respect us and honour the anointing of God upon our lives. They never take us for granted because of familiarity.

As a believer, take a careful study of these people and you will see that it is possible to live very close to a leader or pastor and yet respect them. However, if you notice that the spirit of familiarity has taken you over, make a decision today to break out of its hold and the good Lord will deliver you in Jesus name.

CONCLUSION

Absalom and Ahitophel allowed the spirit of familiarity to lay hold of them against King David. So also did king Saul and Solomon in the later part of their lives got too familiar with God. There were those who never allowed this demon to come between them and their leaders. Samuel did not allow the spirit of familiarity to come between him and Eli even though he had more than enough reasons to disrespect Eli due to his weakness in handling his sons. Samuel knew all one may need to know about the weakness of Eli's family, and despite this he respected and honour him.

Elisha addressed Elijah as 'father' despite all the level of discouragement he had with his mentor when he was about to take up into heaven. This is just to let you know that not every one falls for the demon of familiarity. Some people maintain closeness to their pastor without disrespecting them. I tell you, you can be closed and still have high regards for your leader and pastor. It is a way of doubling the anointing.

Joshua was it all under Moses. When you embark on a marathon fasting, a lot your weakness will be revealed. You become vulnerable. You loose your strength, vigour and physical appeal and your breath begin to stink. Joshua witnesses all of these with his leader including Moses marriage to an Ethiopian woman and his temperament of anger. Yet he did not rebel against him. Please understand that it must have taken discipline on his part. If he had decided to rebel he would have a lot of supporters since it was a well-known fact that the Israelites were not allowed marrying stranger. In spite of all this Joshua respected God's call upon Moses' life.

When you reject the spirit of familiarity and honour your leader regardless of all their fault and shortcomings, it brings you PROMOTION.

Finally, the book of Mathew 24:12 says that in the last day the love of many shall wax cold. Why? It is because of this subtle spirit of familiarity. You will not be a castaway in the Kingdom of God in Jesus name.

Children of God, please pay attention to this demon common to babies in the Lord is fornication, adultery, lying, stealing etc. for mature believer he uses subtle demons like familiarity towards your parents in the Lord, pastor, Word of God, God and Holy Spirit. When you become familiar with your leader, the word of God, the move of the Holy Spirit, etc. You are no more excited about your eternity, you are used to hearing preacher saying: Jesus is coming back again, which you have been hearing since ages and he never showed up so you decided to relax and rest; this is dangerous think about the 5 foolish virgins

The Bible say's in 1st Corinthians 10:12 *"Wherefore let him that thinketh he standeth take heed lest he fall.*

I believe that this message has greatly ministered to you. You will remember at the beginning that I mentioned five spirits that afflicts the saints of God. You will need to flee from the spirit of hypocrisy, self-ego (pride), unforgiveness and overconfidence. These are spirit disturbs your relationship with God and you get stunted in spiritual growth which finally wear you out. You have gone too far with the Lord not to make haven. Do not be off guard. The Lord God shall keep, strengthen and preserve you in Jesus Name.

For those use to my books now, you will kwon that some of these book are a divine instruction or inspiration of God. God gives me these message that can help the body of Christ to be made stronger and focus therefore make all workers to study this and take caution

If your relationship with Christ is not grounded, it is time you make a total commitment to him and rededicated your life to him and his kingdom. Please, read this aloud to God:

Lord Jesus, I repent of my sins. I am sorry to have been too familiar with you. Forgive me and give me another chance to walk with you. Thank you Lord for answering my prayers. Amen.

I counsel you to please give this message to your entire friend so as to discourage this spirit of the last day from afflicting the children of God any further. If you need to contact do that through

E-mail address: prophetmercy13@gmail.com Tell: +2348033055535

May the Lord keep and deliver us from all the wiles of the enemy in Jesus' name. Amen.